TOOL KIT

MAKE IT SMOOTH

Patty Whitehouse

Rourke
Publishing LLC
Vero Beach, Florida 32964

www.rourkepublishing.com

PHOTO CREDITS: © Armentrout: pages 4, 5, 8, 9, 16, 17, 18, 19; © Lynn Stone: pages 7, 10, 11; © Vasko: page 6; © Jim Orr: page 12; © gynane: page 13; © fullvalue: page 14; © gmnicholas: page 15; © zennie: page 20; © saints4757: page 21; © lisafx: page 22

Editor: Robert Stengard-Olliges

Cover design by Nicola Stratford

Library of Congress Cataloging-in-Publication Data

Whitehouse, Patricia, 1958-
 Make it smooth / Patty Whitehouse.
    p. cm. -- (Tool kit)
 Includes index.
 ISBN 1-60044-208-0 (hardcover)
 ISBN 1-59515-562-7 (softcover)
 1. Tools--Juvenile literature. I. Title. II. Series: Whitehouse, Patricia, 1958- Tool kit.
 TJ1195.W5173 2007
 621.9--dc22
                           2006010682

Printed in the USA

CG/CG

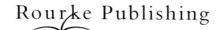

Rourke Publishing

www.rourkepublishing.com – sales@rourkepublishing.com
Post Office Box 3328, Vero Beach, FL 32964

Table of Contents

Making Things Smooth

A **carpenter** wants to use this wood for a table. But it is too rough.

The wood needs to be smooth. The carpenter uses **tools** to make it smooth.

Tools For Work

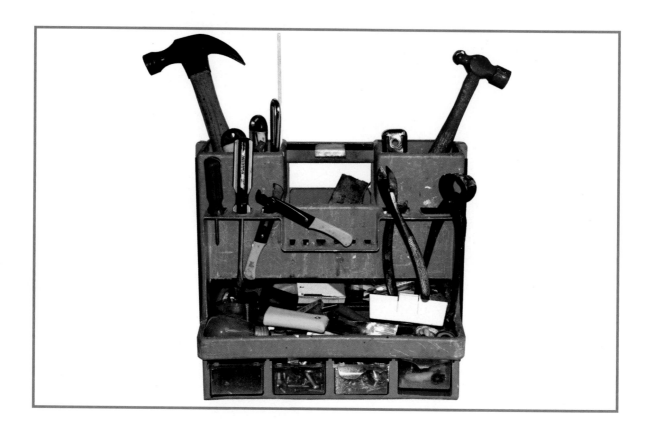

Tools help with many kinds of work. Some tools are for building. Some tools are for growing things.

Tools in this book help make things smooth. Carpenters and other builders use these tools when they work.

Planes

This is a plane. It is a tool for making wood smooth.

Carpenters push a plane across a piece of wood. A **blade** on the plane scrapes the wood to make it smooth.

Files and Rasps

Files are made of **metal**. Files have rows of teeth. They can smooth things made of metal, **plastic** or wood.

Rasps work like files, but have different teeth. Rasps are only for smoothing wood.

Grinders and Sharpeners

This is a grinder. The grinding wheel spins. It makes sparks as it smoothes metal.

This sharpener is for a pencil. It shapes the end of the pencil into a point.

Polishers

A polisher makes things smooth and shiny. It needs electricity to work.

Some polishers use wax to make things shine.
Other polishers scrape things to make them smooth.

Sanders and Sanding Blocks

Sanders smooth wood with sandpaper. Carpenters change the sandpaper when it wears out.

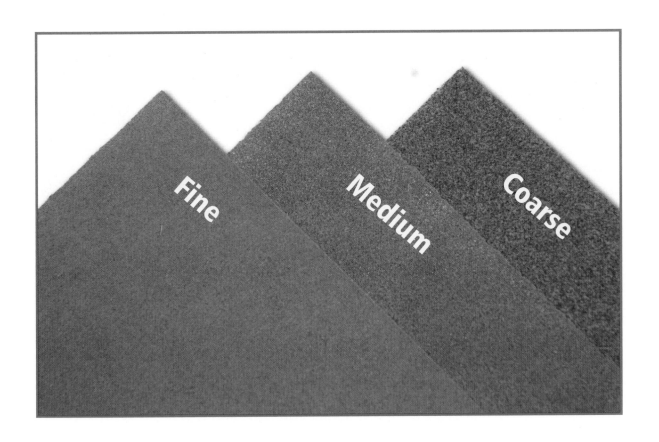

Sandpaper is measured by its **grit**. **Coarse** grit smoothes rough wood. **Fine** grit polishes painted wood.

Bull Floats and Trowels

Concrete needs to be smooth before it hardens. Workers use a bull float to smooth concrete.

A trowel is smaller than a bull float. It makes the concrete smoother than the bull float.

Sandblasters

A sandblaster is used to clean or smooth hard things like bricks and metal. It works like sandpaper.

The bottoms of ships are sandblasted and painted to make them smooth. This helps ships glide through water.

Be Safe With Tools

You should have an adult help you with any tools. You should wear gloves and goggles to protect yourself.

GLOSSARY

blade (BLAYD) — sharp part of a tool

carpenter (KAHR puhn tur) — person who works with wood

coarse (KORSS) — rough sandpaper

concrete (kon KREET) — mixture of rocks and cement used for making sidewalks and roads

fine (FINE) — smooth sandpaper

grit (GRIT) — the feel of sandpaper

metal (MET uhl) — hard, shiny material used to make tools

plastic (PLASS tik) — colorful material that can be formed into tools

tool (TOOL) — something that helps people do work

INDEX

FURTHER READING

Miller, Heather. *Construction Worker.* Heinemann: Chicago, 2002.
Sturges, Philemon. *I Love Tools!.* HarperCollins: New York, 2006.

WEBSITES TO VISIT

www.buildeazy.com/kidsdiy_diyprojects.html
www.thewoodcrafter.net/jr.html
www.enchantedlearning.com/dictionarysubjects/tools.shtml

ABOUT THE AUTHOR

Patty Whitehouse has been a teacher for 17 years. She is currently a Lead Science teacher in Chicago, where she lives with her husband and two teenage children. She enjoys reading, gardening, and writing about science for children.